Still

and Know

Reflections from
Living Buddha, Living Christ

Other Books by Thich Nhat Hanh

Be Still
and Know

Reflections from
Living Buddha, Living Christ

Thich Nhat Hanh

RIVERHEAD BOOKS, NEW YORK

Riverhead Books
Published by The Berkley Publishing Group
200 Madison Avenue
New York, New York 10016

Copyright © 1996 by Thich Nhat Hanh
Book design by Maureen Troy
Cover design by Joe Lanni

All rights reserved. This book, or parts thereof,
may not be reproduced in any form without permission.

First Riverhead edition: October 1996

The Putnam Berkley World Wide Web site address is
http://www.berkley.com/berkley

Library of Congress Cataloging-in-Publication Data

Nhât Hạnh, Thích.
    [Living Buddha, living Christ. Selections]
    Be still and know : reflections from Living Buddha, living Christ
/ Thich Nhat Hanh.
        p.   cm.
    ISBN 1-57322-562-2
    1. Buddhist meditations.   2. Christianity and other religions—
Buddhism.   3. Buddhism—Relations—Christianity.   I. Title.
BQ5572.N432   1996
294.3'443—dc20   96-23336
                                                          CIP

Printed in the United States of America

10   9   8   7   6   5   4   3   2   1

CONTENTS

"Be still and know that I am God."
　　　　　　　　　　　　—Psalm 46

"Be still" means to become peaceful and concentrated. The Buddhist term is *samatha* (stopping, calming). "Know" means to acquire wisdom or understanding. The Buddhist term is *vipasyana* (insight, or looking deeply). When we are still, looking deeply, and touching the source of our true wisdom, we touch the living Buddha and the living Christ in ourselves and in each person we meet.

DIALOGUE

*O*n the altar in my hermitage in France are images of Buddha and Jesus, and every time I light incense, I touch both of them as my spiritual ancestors.

I am able to do this because I have met many real Christians, men and women whose lives and words embody the deepest aspects of the Christian tradition.

∞

*M*ost of the boundaries between traditions are artificial. Truth has no boundaries. The differences are mostly in emphasis.

∞

$\mathcal{D}$o not think the knowledge you presently possess is changeless, absolute truth. Avoid being narrow-minded and bound to present views. Learn and practice nonattachment from views in order to be open to receive others' viewpoints.

∞

When we look into the heart of a flower, we see clouds, sunshine, minerals, time, the earth, and everything else in the cosmos in it. Without clouds, there could be no rain, and there would be no flower.

∞

No single tradition monopolizes the truth. We must glean the best values of all traditions and work together to remove the tensions between them. If we do, peace will have a chance.

∞

For dialogue to be fruitful, we need to live deeply our own tradition and, at the same time, look and listen deeply to others. We can appreciate the beauty and value of our own *and* the other's tradition.

$\mathcal{T}$o stand straight and grow strong, we need roots. After one retreat, a young man told me, "Thây, I feel more Jewish than ever. I will tell my rabbi that a Buddhist monk inspired me to go back to him."

∞

$\mathcal{D}$ialogue must begin, first of all, within oneself. If we cannot make peace within, how can we hope to bring about peace in the world?

∞

True love contains respect. When you practice respect, your love and happiness will continue for a long time.

∞

True love is possible only with understanding.
When there is understanding, compassion is born.

∞

MINDFULNESS AND THE HOLY SPIRIT

The Buddha was asked, "Sir, what do you and your monks practice?" He replied, "We sit, we walk, and we eat." The questioner continued, "But sir, everyone sits, walks, and eats," and the Buddha told him, "When we sit, we *know* we are sitting. When we walk, we *know* we are walking. When we eat, we *know* we are eating." In Buddhism, our effort is to practice mindfulness in each moment—to know what is going on within and all around.

∞

$\mathcal{M}$indfulness is the substance of a Buddha. When you enter deeply into the present moment, you, too, become a living Buddha. You see the nature of reality, and this insight liberates you from suffering and confusion.

∞

To me mindfulness is very much like the Holy Spirit. When you are mindful, you see more deeply, and you can heal the wounds in your own mind through love and understanding. It is not just touching a cloth that brings about a miracle. When you touch deep understanding and love, you are healed.

∞

The Holy Spirit descended on Jesus like a dove, penetrated Him deeply, and He became the manifestation of the Holy Spirit. With the Holy Spirit in Him, Jesus' power as a healer transformed many people. We also have the seed of the Holy Spirit in us—the capacity of healing, transforming, and loving. When we touch that seed, we touch God the Father and God the Son.

∞

$\mathcal{A}$ twelve-year-old boy was asked by his father, "What would you like for your birthday?" The boy replied, "Daddy, I want you!"

His father worked all the time and was rarely at home. His son was a bell of mindfulness, reminding him that the most precious gift we can offer our loved ones is our true presence.

∞

$\mathcal{W}$hen our mindfulness embraces those we love,
they bloom like flowers.

∞

*M*indful speech brings real happiness. Unmindful speech can kill. It doesn't cost anything to use loving speech. Choose your words carefully and you will make many people happy.

∞

We all need something good, beautiful, and true to believe in. Taking refuge in mindfulness, the awareness of what is going on in the present moment, is safe and not at all abstract.

∞

When Buddhists greet one another, we hold our palms together like a lotus flower, breathe in and out mindfully, bow, and say silently, "A lotus for you, a Buddha-to-be." This greeting produces two Buddhas at the same time.

∞

The miracle is not to walk on water. The miracle is to walk on the green earth, dwelling deeply in the present moment and feeling truly alive.

∞

LIVING BUDDHA, LIVING CHRIST

In Crossing the Threshold of Hope, Pope John Paul II says, "If [Christ] were only a wise man like Socrates, if He were a 'prophet' like Muhammed, if He were 'enlightened' like Buddha, without any doubt He would not be what He is. He is the one mediator between God and humanity." Behind this statement is the notion that Christianity provides the only way of salvation and all other religious traditions are of no use. This attitude excludes dialogue and fosters religious intolerance and discrimination. It does not help.

∞

When we read, "The heavens opened and the Holy Spirit descended upon Him like a dove," we can see that Jesus Christ was already enlightened. He was in touch with the reality of life, the source of mindfulness, wisdom, and understanding within Him, and this made Him different from other human beings. When He was born into a carpenter's family, He was the Son of Man. When He opened His heart, the door of Heaven was opened to Him. The Holy Spirit landed Him like a dove, and then He was the Son of God. He became very holy and very great.

*J*esus is the Son of God and the Son of Man. We are all, at the same time, the sons and daughters of God and the children of our parents. This means we are of the same reality as Jesus. This will sound heretical to many Christians, but I believe that theologians who say we are not have to reconsider.

∞

*J*esus lived exactly as he taught, so studying His life is crucial to understanding His teaching. For me, the life of Jesus is His most basic teaching, even more important than faith in the resurrection or faith in eternity.

The lives of the Buddha and Jesus should always be the models for our own practice.

∞

Sitting beneath the Bodhi tree, many wonderful, holy seeds within the Buddha blossomed forth. He was human, but at the same time, he became an expression of the highest spirit of humanity. When we are in touch with the highest spirit in ourselves, we, too, are a Buddha, filled with the Holy Spirit, and we become very open, very deep, and very understanding.

Jesus said, "I am the door"—the door of salvation and everlasting life, the door to the Kingdom of God. Because God the Son is made of the energy of the Holy Spirit, He is the door for us to enter the Kingdom of God.

∞

The Buddha is also described as a door—a teacher who shows us the way in this life. In Buddhism, such a special door is deeply appreciated, but it is said that there are 84,000 other Dharma doors as well, doors of teaching. If you are lucky enough to find a door, it would not be very Buddhist to say that yours is the only door. In fact, we have to open even more doors for future generations.

∞

To encounter a true master is worth a century of studying his or her teaching. In such a person we have a living example of enlightenment, freedom, and peace. How can we encounter a true master? It depends on us. Many who looked directly into the eyes of the Buddha or the eyes of Jesus were not capable of seeing them.

∞

When we see someone overflowing with love and understanding, someone who is deeply aware of what is going on, we know they are very close to the Buddha and to Jesus Christ.

∞

The enlightenment of the Buddha, the compassion and lovingkindness of Jesus, grow every day. We ourselves are responsible for their growth. Our bodies are the continuation of the Buddha's body. Our compassion and understanding are the compassion and understanding of Jesus.

*W*henever I read the stories of Asita and Simeon, the sages who visited the Buddha and Jesus shortly after their births, I wish that every one of us could also be visited by a sage when we are born. The birth of every child is important. We, too, are a Buddha-to-be, a son or daughter of God.

∞

COMMUNITY

*C*hristians have to help Jesus Christ be manifested by their way of life, showing those around them that love, understanding, and tolerance are possible.

∞

$\mathcal{I}$t is not only true that Christians need Jesus, but Jesus also needs Christians for His energy to continue in this world.

When you accidentally strike your finger with a hammer, you take care of the injury immediately. The right hand does not say to the left hand, "I am doing charitable work for you." It just does whatever it can to help—giving first aid, compassion, and concern. This is the spirit of "nonself."

∞

It takes time to practice generosity, but being generous is the best use of our time.

In Christianity, the church is the crown of the path of practice, the true teaching authority. When a church manifests understanding, tolerance, and love, Jesus is there.

∞

$\mathcal{A}$ church that is not filled with the Holy Spirit is not alive.

In East Asia, every home has a family altar. Whenever there is an important event, such as the birth of a daughter or a son going off to college, we announce the news to our ancestors. When we practice this way, we always feel deeply rooted in the family. I encourage those of Western origin to do the same.

∞

$\mathcal{I}$t is much easier to attain stability, joy, and freedom if you practice in community with others.

*E*ven in monasteries, we have to cook, clean, sweep, and wash. Is there a way to do this in a meditative mood? Of course. When we practice mindfulness of cooking, cleaning, sweeping, and washing, we touch the ultimate dimension of reality.

∞

In Buddhist monasteries before every meal, a monk or a nun recites these Five Contemplations: "This food is the gift of the whole universe—the earth, the sky, and much hard work. May we live in a way that is worthy of this food. May we transform our unskillful states of mind, especially that of greed. May we eat only foods that nourish us and prevent illness. May we accept this food for the realization of the way of understanding and love."

∞

*M*indful eating nourishes awareness in us. We needn't be afraid of not having the TV, radio, newspaper, or a complicated conversation while we eat. It is wonderful just to be completely present with our food and those eating with us.

∞

When Buddhists and Christians come together, we should share a meal in mindfulness as a deep practice of Communion. To eat a piece of bread or a bowl of rice mindfully and see that every morsel is a gift of the whole universe is to live deeply. We do not need to distract ourselves from the food, even by listening to scriptures or the lives of bodhisattvas or saints. When mindfulness is present, the Buddha and the Holy Spirit are already there.

∞

PEACE

*W*holesome, spiritual nourishment can be found looking at the blue sky, the spring blossoms, or the eyes of a baby. We can celebrate the joys that are available in these simple pleasures.

∞

$\mathcal{P}$eace is all around us—in the world and in nature—and within us—in our bodies and our spirits. Once we learn to touch this peace, we will be healed and transformed. It is not a matter of faith; it is a matter of practice.

∞

In the *Sermon on the Mount,* Jesus said, "Blessed are the peacemakers: for they shall be called the children of God." Many who work for peace are not at peace. To make peace, our hearts must be at peace with the world. Trying to overcome evil with evil is not working for peace.

We think that if the powerful countries would reduce their weapons arsenals, we could have peace. But if we look deeply into the weapons, we see our own minds—our prejudices, fears, and ignorance. Even if we transport all the bombs to the moon, the roots of war and the roots of the bombs are still here, in our bodies and minds.

∞

Nonviolence does not mean nonaction. Nonviolence means we *act* with love and compassion. The moment we stop acting, we undermine the principle of nonviolence.

∞

*E*ven if our enemy is cruel, even if he is crushing us, sowing terror and injustice, we have to love him. This is the message of Jesus.

How can we love our enemy? The only way is to understand him, to understand how he has come to be the way he is.

∞

In fact, to "love our enemy" is impossible, because the moment we understand him, we feel compassion toward him, and he is no longer our enemy.

People today tend to take refuge in overwork so they can avoid confronting their inner turmoil.

∞

$\mathcal{I}$n each of us, there is nonviolence, and there is also violence. With mindfulness, we can begin to transform the violence, the wars in ourselves, into love, understanding, and compassion.

∞

$\mathcal{A}$. J. Muste said, "There is no way to peace. Peace is the way." We can realize peace right in the present moment with each look, smile, word, and action. Peace is not an end. Each step we take should be peace.

∞

If while we practice, we are not aware that the world is suffering, that children are dying of hunger, that social injustice is going on a little bit everywhere, we are not practicing mindfulness. We are just trying to escape.

∞

Meditation is not a drug to make us oblivious to our real problems. Looking deeply at our own mind and our own life, we begin to see what to do and what not to do to bring about real peace in ourselves and in society.

FAITH AND PRACTICE

*J*esus said, "I am the way." He meant that to have a true relationship with God, you have to practice. Early Christians always spoke of their faith as "the way." To me, "I am the way" is a better statement than "I know the way." The way is not an asphalt road.

∞

We must distinguish between the "I" spoken by Jesus and the "I" that people usually think of. The "I" in His statement is *life* itself. Many who have neither the way nor the life try to impose on others what they believe to be true.

The Buddha said, "If someone is standing on one shore and wants to go to the other shore, he has to either use a boat or swim across. He cannot just wish, 'Oh, other shore, please come over here for me to step across!'" To a Buddhist, prayer without practice is not real prayer.

∞

The living Dharma is mindfulness, manifested in the Buddha's daily life and in your daily life, also. When I see you walking mindfully, I touch the peace, joy, and deep presence of your being. If you are mindful, the living Dharma is easy to recognize.

The place to touch the Kingdom of God is within us. We do not have to die to arrive at the gate of Heaven. In fact, we have to be truly alive. If we touch life deeply enough, the Kingdom of God will become a reality here and now. This is not a matter of devotion. It is a matter of practice.

For monks of old, the secret of success in the practice was to keep the name of Jesus always in mind. The name of Jesus brings the energy of God—the Holy Spirit—into you.

According to Judaism, the entire world, all the good things in life, belong to God, so when we enjoy something, we think of God and enjoy it in His presence. Piety is the recognition that everything is linked to the presence of God in every moment.

∞

When you pray only for good weather for your own picnic and not for the farmers who need the rain, you are doing the opposite of what Jesus taught.

∞

In Buddhism, our source of energy is faith in daily practice. Faith in an *idea* is risky. Ideas can change, and tomorrow we may not believe the same thing. Buddhist faith is experiential. Once we have tasted the reality, no one can remove that from us.

∞

$\mathcal{A}$ life that is too comfortable makes spiritual growth difficult. Food, clothing, and lodging should be adequate, but not excessive.

∞

Thomas Merton wrote, "We must frankly admit that self-denial and sacrifice are absolutely essential to the life of prayer." I understand, although I would not describe a simple life as self-denial or sacrifice. A life of prayer and contemplation can be filled with joy.

∞

UNKNOWABLE GOD

*E*verything Jesus and the Buddha taught was to a particular person or group on a particular occasion. We must try to understand the context in which they spoke in order to understand their meaning. If we just analyze their words, we may miss the point. Theologians sometimes forget this.

∞

The teaching of the Buddha was intended as an instrument for meditation. Since then, many Buddhists have gotten caught by the ideas he presented. They confuse the means and the end, the raft and the shore, the finger pointing to the moon and the moon.

∞

There is something more important than ideas. It is freedom from ideas. For a Buddhist to be attached to any doctrine, even a Buddhist one, is to betray the Buddha.

One Zen Master said to his student, "When you meet the Buddha, kill him!" He meant that the student should kill the *Buddha-concept* in order for him to experience the *real Buddha* directly.

∞

You cannot talk about apple juice to someone who has not tasted it. No matter what you say, the other person will not have the true experience of apple juice. The only way is to drink it.

∞

Reality is quite different from our concepts.

∞

Wittgenstein said, "Concerning that which cannot be talked about, we should not say anything." Theologians spend a lot of time, ink, and breath talking about God. This is talking about what we should not talk about.

∞

$\mathcal{A}$ good theologian says almost nothing about God. The notion of God can keep you from touching God as love, wisdom, and nonfear.

∞

Theologian Paul Tillich said that God is not a person, but also not less than a person. The ultimate dimension of reality has nothing to do with our concepts.

∞

God cannot be experienced through notions and concepts. St. John Chrysostum wrote, "Let us invoke Him as the inexpressible God, incomprehensible, invisible, and unknowable."

∞

If you stick to an idea or an image of God and do not touch the reality of God, one day you will be plunged into the abyss of doubt.

∞

The Kingdom of God is a treasure. Once you have touched that treasure, you know that the things you previously considered to be conditions for your happiness are just obstacles.

∞

Nothing comes from nothing. Before your so-called birth, you already existed in many other forms. Your birthday is really a day of continuation.

∞

In April we cannot see sunflowers in France, so we say the sunflowers do not exist. But the local farmers have already planted thousands of seeds, and when they look at the bare hills, they may be able to see the sunflowers already. The sunflowers *are there*. They lack only the conditions of sun, heat, rain, and July. Just because we cannot see them does not mean that they do not exist.

When St. Francis asked the almond tree to tell him about God, immediately the tree was covered with beautiful flowers. It was winter. There were no leaves, flowers, or fruits, but he saw the flowers.

The greatest relief is to touch the ultimate dimension of reality. Once you are capable of touching the ocean's water, you will not be afraid of the being and nonbeing as well as the coming and going of the waves.

∞

$\mathcal{U}$nderstanding and love are values that transcend dogma.

∞

$\mathcal{F}$or information about Thich Nhat Hanh's retreat community in France, please contact:

Plum Village
Meyrac
47120 Loubès-Bernac, France

For a complete list of books and tapes by Thich Nhat Hanh and a schedule of his retreats and lectures worldwide, contact:

Parallax Press
P.O. Box 7355
Berkeley, California 94707
World Wide Web: http://www.parallax.org

$\mathcal{A}$ rare combination of mystic, scholar, and activist, Vietnamese monk **Thich Nhat Hanh** is one of the most beloved Buddhist teachers in the West. Poet, Zen master, and chairman of the Vietnamese Buddhist Peace Delegation during the Vietnam War, he was nominated by Dr. Martin Luther King, Jr., for the Nobel Peace Prize. He is the author of thirty books, including *Peace Is Every Step*.